The Rise of the Sauropods

Jon Hughes

Contents

Introducing the Sauropods   2
Discovering the 'Thunder Lizard'   4
Before the Sauropods   6
The Jurassic Period: Rise of the Sauropods   12
What a Sauropod Looked Like   18
How Did Sauropods Live?   26
Sauropod Nests   28
The Last of the Sauropods   30
Why Did the Sauropods Die Out?   32
Could a Sauropod Have Survived?   34
Sauropod Sizes   36
Glossary   38
Index   39

Introducing the Sauropods

The sauropods were the biggest animals ever to walk the Earth. They were a type of dinosaur that lived in a warm, wet climate, between 150 and 70 million years ago. Sauropods had huge bodies and very long necks. Their tails were even longer. Some were as long as a small airliner, and weighed as much as seven elephants.

TRIASSIC PERIOD	JURASSIC PERIOD	
Dinosaurs, mammals evolve	Birds evolve	MESOZOIC
248 million years ago	206 million years ago	144 million years ago

CRETACEOUS PERIOD		CENOZOIC	
Dinosaurs become extinct			People evolve
	65 million years ago		Now

Discovering the 'Thunder lizard'

In 1879, American scientist Othniel Charles Marsh discovered the sauropod. He found the **fossilised** bones of a huge, **extinct** animal. He arranged these into a skeleton and found that the animal had a large body. It had four strong legs, a long neck and a tail. However, its head was small.

Marsh realized that this animal would have been very big and very heavy. It would have made the ground shake as it walked. So, he named it 'Brontosaurus' (bron-tuh-sawr-us). This means 'Thunder Lizard' in Greek.

This picture of a brontosaurus skeleton was drawn in 1896.

Fact File
Lizard Feet

Many people still call all long-necked dinosaurs "brontosaurs", but the correct name for this type of animal is a sauropod (sawr-oh-pod), meaning "lizard-footed".

HOW DO SCIENTISTS KNOW?

FOSSILS

1) An animal dies.

2) The skeleton is covered in sand and mud.

3) As time passes, more layers of sand and mud form and cover the skeleton.

4) Over millions of years, the fossils are formed.

5) Weather wears down the rocks and the fossils are revealed on the surface.

CRETACEOUS PERIOD — Dinosaurs become extinct — 65 million years ago — CENOZOIC — People evolve — Now

Before the Sauropods

Pangea

230 million years ago, Earth looked very different than it does today. Countries and **continents** were clumped together to form one large **landmass**. This was called Pangea. The **climate** was much warmer than nowadays.

The middle of Pangea was made up of deserts. Near the coast, it was much wetter. Rainy seasons made lakes and rivers, and jungles were formed.

TRIASSIC PERIOD
Dinosaurs, mammals evolve
248 million years ago

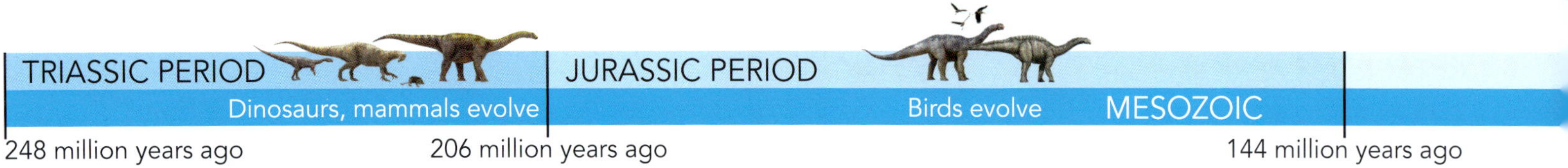

JURASSIC PERIOD
206 million years ago

Birds evolve   MESOZOIC
144 million years ago

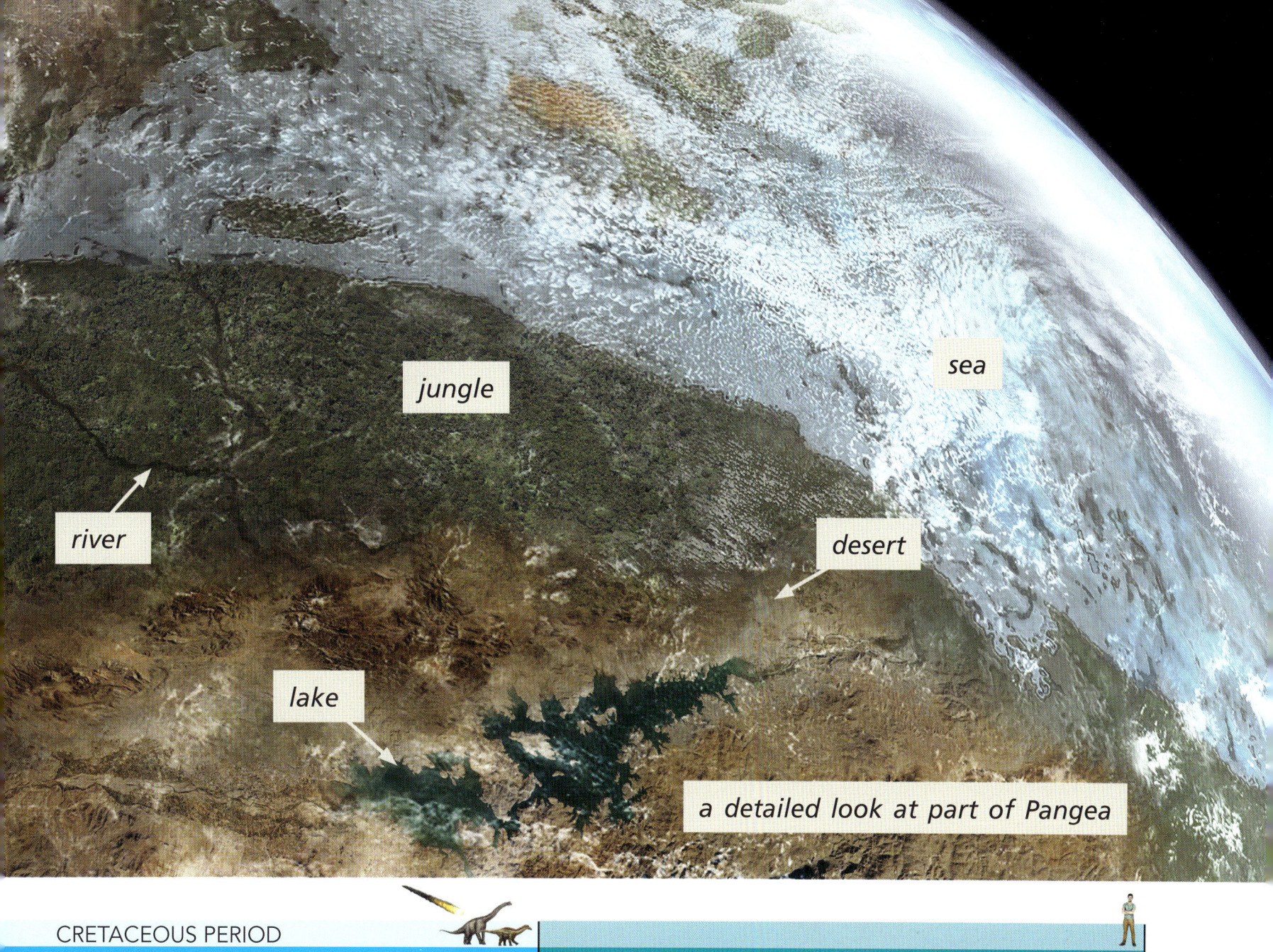

Scientists think that sauropods developed from much smaller animals. Their ancestors were called prosauropods (pro-sawr-oh-pods). This means 'before the lizard-footed'. The earliest remains of prosauropods date back tens of millions of years before brontosaurus and the other sauropods even existed.

Fact File

The oldest dinosaur fossils ever found were a pair of prosauropod jaw bones. They were found in Madagascar in 1999.

TRIASSIC PERIOD	JURASSIC PERIOD	MESOZOIC
Dinosaurs, mammals evolve	Birds evolve	
248 million years ago	206 million years ago	144 million years ago

This animal is a Prosauropod. Prosauropod fossils are over 228 million years old. They are the earliest dinosaur fossils ever found.

CRETACEOUS PERIOD

Dinosaurs become extinct

65 million years ago

CENOZOIC

People evolve

Now

Prosauropods also had long necks, long tails and small heads. Their jaws were filled with small peg-like teeth. They usually walked around on four legs, but they were able to stand up on their back legs to reach leaves growing up high.

Fact File

Prosauropods were herbivores. This means that they ate plants and did not eat meat.
They were so big, they had to keep eating all day.

Plateosaurus (play-tee-oh-saw-rus) standing up on its back legs to eat

The Jurassic Period: Rise of the Sauropods.

Over 80 million years, Pangea moved and split apart to form new continents. At the same time, it got hotter and wetter. Jungles covered the landscape. They provided enough food for all kinds of herbivores, including dinosaurs.

TRIASSIC PERIOD — Dinosaurs, mammals evolve
248 million years ago

JURASSIC PERIOD — Birds evolve   MESOZOIC
206 million years ago   144 million years ago

The volcanoes made the climate change. More plants could grow so there was more food for the sauropods.

CRETACEOUS PERIOD | Dinosaurs become extinct | 65 million years ago | CENOZOIC | People evolve | Now

Other animals lived alongside the sauropods. Flying reptiles called pterosaurs flew between the trees, hunting insects.

Other species of dinosaurs roamed the landscape. Some of these were **carnivores**. They hunted the animals that lived in and around the forests.

Fact File
Pterosaurs

There were many different types of pterosaur. Some were small and ate insects. Others caught birds and small animals.

Sauropods, like these apatosaurs, roamed alongside carnivorous dinosaurs. They were usually too big to be eaten.

About 144 million years ago, there were many different species of sauropod. They had very few predators. This was because they were bigger than most of the other animals living around them.

Supersaurus, (soo-per-sawr-us) meaning 'super lizard', was 34 metres long and 8 metres high, and weighed as much as 70 tons.

Supersaurus was twice as high as a large African elephant and seven times heavier.

CRETACEOUS PERIOD | Dinosaurs become extinct | 65 million years ago | CENOZOIC | People evolve | Now

17

What a Sauropod Looked Like

The sauropods had huge stomachs because they had to eat almost all the time. They had many metres of intestines to process all the plants they ate.

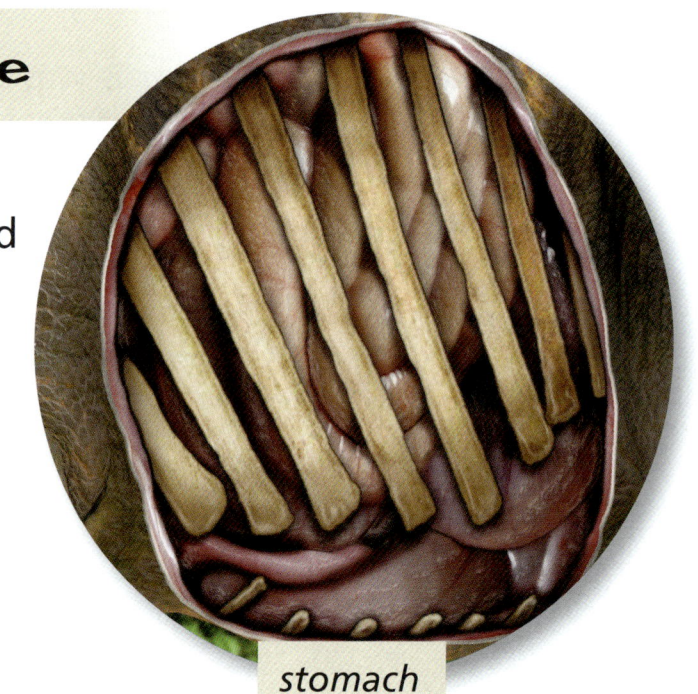

stomach

The sauropods could reach vegetation easily because of their long necks. They swept them from side to side to gather branches and leaves. They could do this without having to move the rest of their body.

Sauropods had small heads. This meant that their necks could grow longer without having to carry a heavy skull at the end. The small size also meant they could reach between the branches to get to the leaves they wanted to eat. Then they used their sharp, peg-like teeth to strip the leaves from the branches.

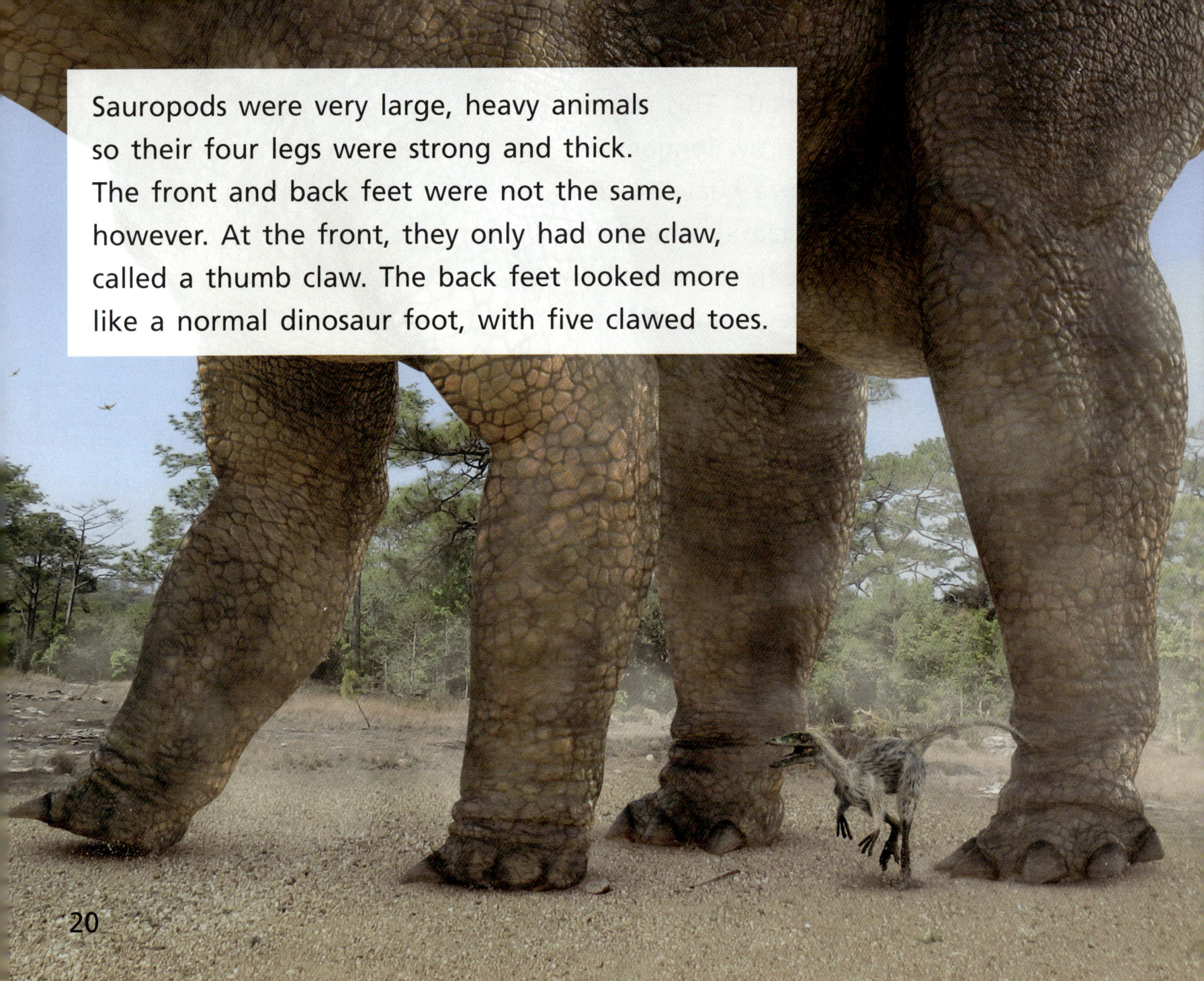

Sauropods were very large, heavy animals so their four legs were strong and thick. The front and back feet were not the same, however. At the front, they only had one claw, called a thumb claw. The back feet looked more like a normal dinosaur foot, with five clawed toes.

HOW DO SCIENTISTS KNOW?

SKIN

Sometimes, the pattern on a dinosaur's skin becomes a fossil in rock. Scientists can see what dinosaur's looked like.

fossilised imprint of dinosaur skin

Some sauropods grew bony **armour** on their thick skin to defend them against attacks. Others could fight off attackers using other parts of their bodies. The shunosaurus, for example, grew spikes on the ends of its tail. It used its tail like a **club** to swing at attacking predators.

The diplodocus (di-plod-u-kus) had a tough, thin and flexible end to its tail. It could use it as a whip against animals attacking it.

a diplodocus protecting itself with its tail

How Did Sauropods Live?

Many types of sauropod lived in herds. This helped them defend themselves against the carnivorous dinosaurs that hunted them. Moving around in groups confused predators because they didn't know which one to attack. Being in a group also protected the young animals. They stayed in the centre of the group, surrounded by the bigger adults.

HOW DO SCIENTISTS KNOW?

MOVING

The fossilised tracks of dinosaurs have been found all over the world. These footprints help scientists tell how an animal moved, how fast it travelled and what its feet looked like.

fossilised tracks

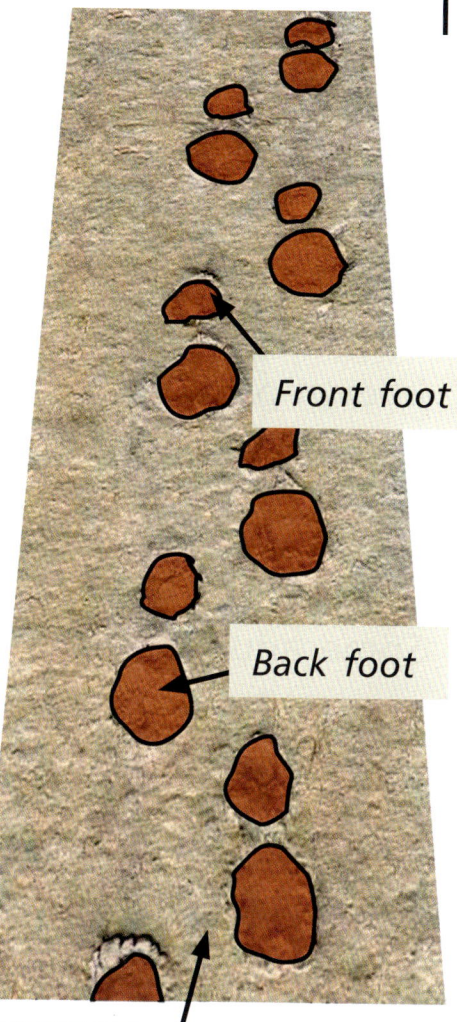

Direction of travel

Front foot

Back foot

The narrow spaces between footprints show the legs came straight down from the body. There are no tail marks. This shows the dinosaur held its tail off the ground.

Sauropod Nests

Sauropods laid eggs in shallow rounded pits on the ground. These nests were called scrapes. They were made in large groups, in areas known as nest sites. Females laid between 15 and 40 eggs each. The eggs were arranged in rows or **clutches**. Some adults may have guarded their nests. Others just covered up their eggs with soil and left them. Most of the eggs never hatched, but so many eggs were laid by each female that enough **hatchlings** survived to grow into adults.

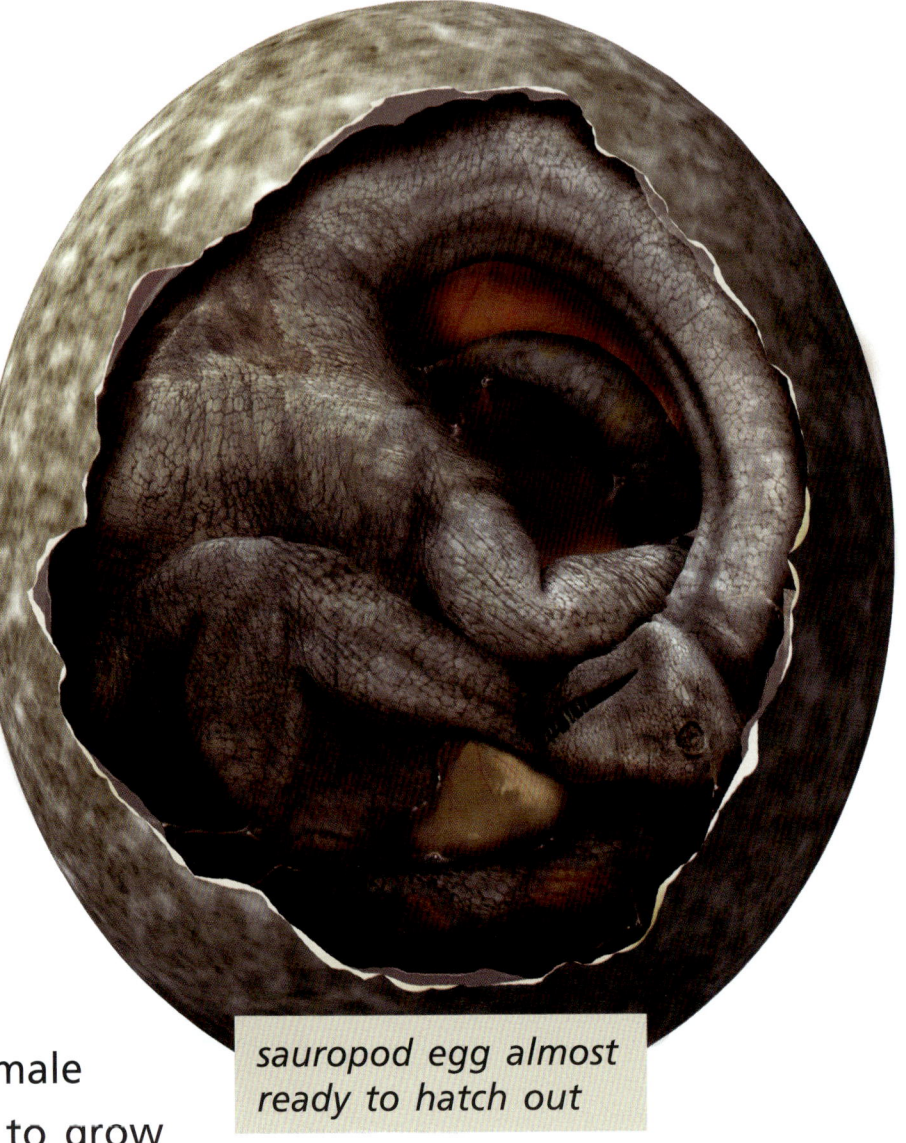

sauropod egg almost ready to hatch out

HOW DO SCIENTISTS KNOW?

NESTS

In 1997, scientists found one of the largest dinosaur nesting sites in the world. The thousands of fossilised eggs and nests discovered belonged to a type of sauropod species called titanosaurus. It was one of the largest animals to have walked the earth.

The Last of the Sauropods

Sauropods were larger than other animals that lived around them. Magyarosaurus (ma-gee-a-row-saw-rus) was one of the smallest sauropods at about 6 metres long. It was still bigger than other animals living nearby. It measured about 6 metres long.

Just over 65 million years ago, one main type of sauropod, called titanosaurus, was found all over the world. It was the largest of all dinosaurs and had a similar body shape to the earlier sauropods.

CRETACEOUS PERIOD — Dinosaurs become extinct — 65 million years ago | CENOZOIC — People evolve — Now

Why Did the Sauropods Die Out?

The last of the sauropods died out at the same time as most of the other dinosaurs. This happened about 65 million years ago.

Fact File

It is thought a huge asteroid crashed into the earth. This caused the extinction of many species, including the sauropods.

TRIASSIC PERIOD
Dinosaurs, mammals evolve
248 million years ago

JURASSIC PERIOD
206 million years ago

Birds evolve   MESOZOIC
144 million years ago

HOW DO SCIENTISTS KNOW?

ASTEROIDS

Scientists have found a layer of clay in rocks that occurs all over the world. It was laid down at the same time and they call this layer 'The KT Boundary'. This clay contains a mineral called Iridium. It is very rare here on earth, but is quite common in **asteroids**.

CRETACEOUS PERIOD

Dinosaurs become extinct

65 million years ago

CENOZOIC

People evolve

Now

Could a Sauropod have Survived?

It would be fantastic to think that somewhere in the world, in a lost valley deep in a jungle, dinosaurs are still surviving.

Animals that were once believed to be extinct have been found again. For many years now, fishermen in remote jungle areas sometimes say they have seen a large, dangerous animal. They call it 'Mokele-mbembe.' This means 'one who stops the flow of rivers'. The way they describe this animal is very similar to the old drawings of the Brontosaurus: a big body, long neck with small head, and a long tail dragging on the ground. Despite many expeditions over the past 100 years, no one has ever found this animal. But people keep on looking.

A fisherman seeing what he thinks is Mokele-mbembe. It is very unlikely that a sauropod could have survived millions of years in the jungles of Africa.

CRETACEOUS PERIOD — Dinosaurs become extinct — 65 million years ago

CENOZOIC — People evolve — Now

Sauropod Sizes

- saturnalia
- magyarosaurus
- plateosaurus
- shunosaurus
- brontosaurus

Glossary

armour	hard, protective layer on the outside
asteroids	small rocks going round the sun
carnivores	meat-eating animals
club	something heavy used as a weapon
clutches	small group of eggs laid at the same time
dinosaur	prehistoric reptile
extinct	no longer living
fossilised	preserved in rock, leaving a print of the living animal or plant
hatchlings	young animals that have recently come out of their shells
landmass	large area of land in one piece
predators	animals that kill and eat other animals
skeleton	framework of bone, supporting the body of an animal

Index

armour   22, 38

asteroid   22, 38

bone   4, 8, 22

carnivore   14, 38

club   22, 38

egg   28-29, 38

fossil   4-5, 8-9, 21, 27, 29

Pangea   6-7, 12

predator   16, 22, 26, 38

skelton   4, 5, 38

White band

The Rise of the Sauropods — Jon Hughes
Teaching notes written by Sue Bodman and Glen Franklin

Using this book

Developing reading comprehension
This non-fiction text is predominantly written in the report genre, with elements of procedural text (p.5) and explanatory text in the 'How do scientists know?' sections (pp.21, 27, 29 and 33). The reader is taken from the discovery of the fossilised remains of a sauropod, through the development of early sauropods to the events that led to the extinction of the dinosaurs. This book has some complex ideas, including the use of technical vocabulary of time periods. The timeline at the bottom of the pages supports the reader's understanding of the passing of time.

Grammar and sentence structure
- Sentence structures are longer, and include subordinate phrases or clauses, for example: *'When he arranged these into a skeleton, he discovered that the animal had a large body'* (p.4).
- Sentences are written as appropriate to a report text using a generic style and present tense verbs.

Word meaning and spelling
- Language of size and shape is detailed, for example *'peg-like teeth'* (p.10), *'tough, thin and flexible end'* (p.24).
- Unfamiliar language is used. This gives an opportunity to reinforce word-reading skills on unfamiliar words and technical vocabulary.

Curriculum links
Science – P.27 explains how footprints can be analysed to tell the size shape and direction of travel. Collect some images of footprints and write a simple report about what can be discerned about the animal from the shape and location of the footprint.

Art – Use modelling clay to create sculptures of Sauropods. The book provides detailed information about the features that can inform some detailed work.

Learning outcomes
Children can:
- tackle unfamiliar words, and monitor their own understanding
- search for and find information in texts, using a range of non-fiction text features
- sustain interest across a longer text, employing comprehension strategies to enable them to return to it after a break.

A guided reading lesson

Book Introduction
Give each child a book. Ask them to read the title and blurb quietly to themselves. Say: *This text is called 'The Rise of the Sauropods'. What do you think 'Rise' means here?* Establish meaning of the word in the title and how that relates to the development of the species.

Orientation
Ask the group to share what they think the text will be about. Discuss their knowledge of dinosaurs in general – they may have read other reports on dinosaurs (or even *'Pterosaurs'* in Purple Band of Cambridge Reading Adventures). Then say: *Today we are going to read about a particular type of dinosaur. They were massive. They lived for a very long time.*

Preparation
Turn to pages 2 and 3. Point out how this introductory page in setting the purpose of the book. Support vocabulary of the vast time periods involved by examining the timeline, noting that the line moves from left to right, getting closer to present day. Read the complex words representing time periods aloud and encourage the children practise saying them.

Look at the picture and draw out language to describe the sauropod that includes content from pages later in the book – long necks, small head, heavy back legs, smaller front legs, armoured skin, spikes, long, thin tail, for example. This will support the children later in the book.